Albert and the runaway train

The Adventures of Albert Mouse
Book Four

James Hywel

OINK
BOOKS

Written for

Morgan & Josie

and

Mr Spike

Albert Books

The mouse who wanted to see the world

Albert and the smuggler Mickey Mustard

Albert takes to the sky

Albert and the runaway train

Albert buys a boat

Albert learns to swim

Albert and the Newcomen Engine

Chapter 1

There was some excitement in No. 10 Higher Street. In fact, there hadn't been this much excitement since Albert and Big Tony had helped the police catch the notorious smuggler, Mickey Mustard.

What was the cause of all this excitement, you may ask? Well, it was because Albert's Grandma Bramble was coming to stay for Christmas and she was due to arrive later that day. Grandma Bramble lives in the Highlands of Scotland and the last time she visited

Dartmouth was when Albert had been born.

Of everyone in the house, Albert was the most excited. Thanks to his reward money for catching Mickey Mustard, he had been able to buy her a First Class train ticket so she could visit them.

The entire house had woken up very early, so early in fact that the sun hadn't even risen over the fields behind Kingswear.

After Albert had finished his morning exercises and cleaned his teeth, he quickly dressed in his best white shirt, matching trousers and waistcoat. He even put on his favourite red bow tie.

"Perfect!" he said, looking at himself in the mirror.

Albert picked up his flat cap.

"Now it's time for breakfast."

Chapter 2

Downstairs, Mrs Mouse had assigned everyone a job. Dorothy and Millie were tidying their rooms and putting all their toys neatly away. While they were doing that, their mother was busy cleaning and dusting everything. The house wasn't especially dirty, but she knew that Grandma Bramble was very particular and would see the smallest speck of dust.

"Albert!" shouted his mother. "Are you up and dressed yet?"

"Coming!" replied Albert as he slid down the bannister rail, and shot into the air, doing several summersaults before landing on his feet on the hallway floor.

"I'm ready," he said, walking into the kitchen, where his mother was cleaning the window.

His mother turned round and looked at her son.

"Don't you look smart," she said. "Now, you remember the time of the train, don't you?"

"Yes, Mum, I remember," said Albert.

"And you know it's platform one?"

"Yes, Mum, I have the piece of paper you gave me last night with everything written down on it," sighed Albert, patting his pocket.

"I'm just making sure, that's all. You know how Grandma will be if you're late?"

"Yes, I know, you told me," said the little mouse as he sat down at the table to eat his breakfast.

"How come we have to clean while Albert gets to go into town?" asked Dorothy, coming into the kitchen.

"Because Albert's job is to meet Grandma off the train and bring her safely here," said her mother.

"I could do that!" said Dorothy.

"No you couldn't," said Albert, taking a bite of his cheese sandwich. "Only I know where the train station is. You haven't even been beyond the garden gate."

"Well, it can't be difficult, all you have to do is look for a train," said Dorothy. "Anyway, you only know where the station is because you flew over it when you were carried away on those balloons and nearly died!"

"That was a controlled flight and I didn't nearly die for your information," said Albert crossly.

"That's enough you two. Albert is going to the station and that's that!" said Mrs Mouse.

Chapter 3

After Albert had finished his breakfast he washed his hands and cleaned his whiskers.

"Right, I'm off," he said.

"Ok. You will be careful out there, won't you?"

"Yes, Mum," sighed Albert.

"Always remember to look twice before crossing the roads," said his mother. "And please don't stop to talk to sign autographs and have photos taken, otherwise you will be late."

"I know," sighed the little mouse.

"You're sure you'll be ok on the ferry? Remember to hold on tight."

"I'll be fine, Mum," said Albert as he hugged his mother.

The little mouse walked down the garden path, waved to his mother, squeezed under the gate and was gone.

"Oh, I do hope he will be alright," said Mrs Mouse looking worried.

"He'll be fine," said Millie, holding her mother's hand.

"As long as he doesn't fall off the ferry and have to be rescued by the lifeboat again," said Dorothy.

"Please don't say that! He's just so small and with all those cars and people, I worry so much," said Mrs Mouse, as she stepped back inside the house and closed the front door.

Chapter 4

As Albert waited to cross the road outside his house, he saw Mrs Saunders unlocking the door to the bookshop.

"Hello, Albert. You're looking very smart this morning, off anywhere special?" she asked.

"Good morning, Mrs Saunders. I'm going to the train station to meet my Grandma who is arriving from Scotland," replied Albert, feeling very proud.

"Oh my, that is a long journey for her. When she has recovered from her trip you must bring her over to the shop so I can meet her."

"I will, anyway, I'd better be going, I have to catch the ferry," said Albert and he dashed across the road.

The little mouse decided to take the shortcut between the Old Chantry at No.11 and the Cherub Inn to save some time.

"Morning, Albert," said Clare, who was putting the empty barrels outside the pub ready for collection. "Gosh, you do look smart today."

"Morning, Clare. I'm meeting my Grandma at the train station. I'd like to stop and talk but I have to catch the ferry. I'll bring my Grandma over to meet you when she's rested."

"That would be lovely. Nice to see you, Albert," said Clare, as Albert leapt down the flight of steps that led onto Fairfax Place.

At the bottom of the steps, the little mouse turned right into Lower Street.

"Morning, Albert!" said a lady at Diartt Gallery who was watering two little trees outside her shop.

Albert waved politely.

A child tugged at her mother's arm on the other side of the street.

"Mum, is that Albert Mouse?" she asked her in a whisper, pointing to Albert.

The lady turned and looked at the little mouse, who had now stopped to have his photo taken with a group of children outside Cafe Alf Resco.

"I think it is, but he's smaller than I expected," said the child's mother.

Albert signed a few autographs and then headed towards the small road that led down to the ferry.

Chapter 5

A few other people were already waiting on the slipway when Albert arrived. He could see the ferry slowly making its way back across the estuary from Kingswear.

Several people recognised Albert and waved hello.

Eventually, the ferry arrived so Albert and the small crowd of people moved aside to let the cars drive off. Then the ferryman gave the all-clear for everyone to walk onto the ferry.

"Morning, Albert," said the captain of the Tom Casey as he saw the little mouse. "Where might you be off to today?"

"I'm meeting my Grandma who is arriving by train this morning," said Albert, as he took a neatly folded five-pound note out of his pocket that his mother had given him and held it out to the captain.

The ferry captain shook his head.

"I'm not taking your money, Albert. My grandson will be most upset if I charge you, but if you could just sign this piece of paper for him, that would be marvellous," said the captain.

Albert took the paper and pen and signed his name.

"There you go. Thank you very much," said Albert, putting the money back in his pocket.

The ferryman then collected the fares from the other passengers.

"How come the rodent didn't have to pay?" asked a grumpy-looking man who was obviously a tourist.

The Captain of the Tom Casey looked sternly at the man.

"That there is no rodent. That's Albert Mouse and you will show him some respect or I'll be throwing you off this ferry and you can swim across to Kingswear."

The grumpy man paid his fare and said no more.

Just then a large gull glided down and sat on the railings of the ferry next to Albert.

"I see the tourists are as rude as ever," said the gull.

"Oh, hello Big Tony!" replied Albert.

"So, where are you off to looking all dressed up?" asked Big Tony.

"Have you forgotten, my grandma is arriving from Scotland today?" said the mouse.

"Oh, that's today, is it? I thought it was next week. Anyway, we have a massive problem that I need to talk to you about."

"Has Mickey Mustard returned from South America?" asked the mouse.

"Worse than that. I'm being impersonated!" said Big Tony.

"Impersonated?" asked Albert.

"It's when someone pretends to be someone else......," said the gull.

"I know what it means," interrupted Albert.

"So why did you ask me what it meant? Anyway, the thing is it seems that......,"

Before Big Tony could finish explaining what was wrong the grumpy man who had been rude about Albert spoke again.

"I suppose the seagull isn't going to have to pay either?" he asked in a very loud voice.

"Right, that's it," said Big Tony, turning to the man. "What's your problem?"

"My problem is 'free-loaders' like you and the rat getting a free ferry ride when the rest of us have to pay, that's my problem," said the grumpy man.

"Ignore him, Big Tony, it's not worth having an argument," said Albert.

The gull tried to calm himself down but the man spoke again.

"What, nothing to say?" said the man, turning to the passengers. "I thought it was a seagull, but obviously it's a chicken!"

The man laughed and made 'clucking' noises like a chicken.

Big Tony had heard enough, so he lept down off the railing and walked across to the man.

"I've just about had enough of you," he said. "I'm no chicken, and my friend over there is no rat."

"Ah, so you fight the rat's battles for him, do you?"

"Listen, pal. Albert is not a rat and if you say it again I'm going to have to give you a proper smack!"

Almost immediately the captain came over.

"It's ok, Big Tony, I'll deal with this," he said.

The captain turned to the grumpy man.

"I'm not letting you insult my passengers, especially Albert and Big Tony, so I'm going to have to ask you to leave my ship. NOW!"

"Hey, I was only joking," said the man, now realising he was in a bit of trouble.

"OFF!" said the captain in a loud voice and pointed back towards the slipway.

The man slowly walked to the end of the ferry and stepped back onto the slipway.

"There, that's better. Sorry about that, Big Tony," said the Captain.

"It's ok, but I could have sorted him out myself," said the gull.

Slowly the ferry pulled off the slipway and headed across the water towards Kingswear, leaving the grumpy man alone on the slipway.

Chapter 6

Big Tony hopped back onto the railing next to Albert.

"Now, where was I?" he asked.

"You were telling me about this problem you have," said Albert.

"Yes, thank you. The thing is several people in Dartmouth have also been calling themselves 'Big Tony' and I'm not having it!"

"Really, like who?" asked Albert.

"The Rat with a wooden leg, and that sparrow. Then there's the pigeon, you know, the one that's always seen at the market. Oh, and the dog that lives down Smith Street, near the butchers," said the gull, folding his arms.

Albert thought for a moment and suddenly remembered having met all these people when he'd been on his first adventure to see the whole world.

"Oh, I know them! But I thought they were all really called Big Tony, just like you?"

"No, they're not. The rat's name is Reginald or 'Reg' to his friends. The sparrow is Stuart 'Stu'. The pigeon's real name is Pete....,"

The gull paused and looked at Albert.

"Hang on. You know these people!?" asked Big Tony.

"Well, I wouldn't say I know them exactly. I may have met them in passing once.....," said Albert, feeling slightly embarrassed.

"May have met them in passing when exactly?" asked Big Tony, folding his wings across his chest.

"When I was going to see the world. I bumped into them on the way. They were all very helpful, even Big Tony the dog."

"His name isn't Big Tony, it's Desmond! You know what, Albert, I thought you were my friend and now I find out that you knew about all this and you didn't tell me."

"Now hang on a second. They said their names were Big Tony and I just thought that it was a common name.....,"

"Common?" stuttered the gull, looking hurt.

"I didn't mean that...," said Albert, realising he had hurt his friend's feelings.

"Well, it's what you just said. You said I was common."

"What I meant was that I just didn't think there was anything odd when they said their name was Big Tony, that's all," said Albert.

"I'm very disappointed, Albert, I have to say."

"Look, Big Tony, I'm very sorry. If I'd known that they were using your name, I would have told you, I promise," said the little mouse, looking as sorry as he could. "Anyway, why would they say their name was Big Tony if it wasn't?"

"To elevate their status in the neighbourhood by using my good name," said the gull.

Just then the ferry jolted as it bumped up against the slipway in Kingswear.

"Welcome to Kingswear!" shouted the captain, opening the gates to let the passengers off. "Mind the step and watch yourself on the slope, it's a little slippy."

Chapter 7

Albert and Big Tony waited as they let the other passengers off the ferry first.

"Thank you very much," said Albert, shaking the captain's hand.

"My pleasure. I'll see you both on the return journey," said the captain.

Albert and Big Tony walked up to the station.

"So, what have you got to say?" asked Big Tony.

"About what?" replied Albert.

"About these people pretending to be me, that's what!"

"Well, I'm not an expert, but I don't think there is a law against it is there?" said Albert as he went into the station.

"I've asked around and I'm reliably informed there is a law if you must know," said the gull, looking at Albert. "You're not listening, are you?"

"I am, but I just need to check the arrival time of the train," said the little mouse as he looked up at the noticeboard.

The lady at the ticket counter leant over and looked at Albert and Big Tony.

"Hello, Albert, nice to have you visiting us today," she said.

"I'm here to meet my Grandma," said Albert. "Is the train on time?"

"I'm afraid the train is slightly delayed. Well, when I say delayed, what I mean is it hasn't even left here yet," said the lady.

"What!?" asked Albert, looking through the doors at Platform No. 1, where the shiny green steam train No. 5239, with the brass plaque that said 'GOLIATH' in large letters, was waiting.

"Oh, no. Does that mean my Grandma is still in Paignton?"

"Yes, I'm afraid it does, but if you like, I can give you a free ticket so you can get on this train and then meet your Grandma in Paignton?" said the kind lady.

"Could you really? Wow, that would be amazing!" said the little mouse. "But I'm actually with my friend here. Do you know Big Tony?"

"Of course I do. Here you go, two return tickets to Paignton," she said. "But run, I think it's leaving any second."

Albert took the tickets, and then he and Big Tony ran across the platform to the waiting train.

Chapter 8

Just as Albert and Big Tony sat down in their seats the man on the platform blew his whistle and the large steam train slowly pulled out of the station.

"Isn't this exciting, Big Tony? I don't suspect you thought we'd be having a ride on a real steam train this morning, did you?" said Albert.

Big Tony didn't answer. He was still thinking about his problem.

Just then there was an announcement by the train driver.

"Good morning, everyone, this is your driver speaking. I'd like to apologise for the delay in your journey this morning. We will try to make up for the delay. I'd also like to welcome two very special passengers on board this morning. Albert Mouse and Big Tony are travelling with us today. Next stop - Paignton."

"Isn't this exciting!" said Albert again. "I just wish my mother was here as well. One day I'll arrange for her to have a trip on this train. She'll love it."

Albert gazed out of the window.

"Can we please get back to my problem?" asked Big Tony who didn't seem too excited by the train.

"Problem?" asked Albert.

"The impersonators! You know what, Albert, I don't think you are really listening to me at all," said Big Tony.

"I'm sorry," said Albert, turning away from the window. "I am. So what are you going to do about it?"

"I'm going to take them to court, that's what I'm going to do. I'm not having them using my name to get free stuff," said the gull.

"Free stuff?' asked Albert looking confused.

"Yes, free stuff. Just imagine if Desmond the dog had got on the ferry this morning pretending to be me. He would have got a free trip. Then if Reg Rat had arrived at the train station he would have been given a free ticket and would now be sitting here instead of me."

Albert thought for a moment.

"I really don't think things like that could happen, after all, doesn't everyone know you are a gull and not a dog or rat with one wooden leg?"

"Yes, but what if they didn't? Take that grumpy tourist man for instance. He didn't know who you or I were. If Des or Reg were on the ferry and said their names were Big Tony, then he would have believed them."

"Well, I really don't think that is going to happen," said Albert.

"The point is, it could, and if it did, then those impostors would be getting all my free stuff instead of me," said Big Tony.

"I suppose."

"There is no suppose about it, my friend. I feel like I've been robbed. Robbed of the stuff I've never been given yet, and that's the worst kind of robbery," said Big Tony.

Just then there was another announcement from the train driver.

"Good morning, everyone, this is your driver speaking. We will shortly be arriving in Paignton. I'd like to apologise for the delay in your journey this morning, but I'd like to thank you for travelling with the Dartmouth Steam Railway and River Boat Company. Next stop - Paignton."

"That didn't take us long," said Albert jumping down from his seat. "I hope my Grandma hasn't been waiting too long."

Chapter 9

Albert and Big Tony stepped off the train onto the platform and looked around, but neither of them could see Albert's grandma.

"What does she look like?" asked Big Tony.

"A mouse, like me, obviously," said Albert.

"Oh, right," said the gull.

Just then a man dressed in a station uniform stepped toward them.

"Albert Mouse and Big Tony, I'd like to welcome you both to Paignton Station."

Albert shook the man's hand.

"I'm actually here to meet my Grandma, she is arriving from Scotland but we are a bit late. She will be very worried."

"That's all been taken care of. We've taken your Grandma to the station coffee shop. Kingswear Station telephoned us to say you were on your way so we've made your grandmother as comfortable as we can. She's had us all in fits of laughter. She is a very funny lady.

She's been showing us lots of photos of you as a baby," said the man.

"Just wonderful," sighed Albert.

"Oh, I can't wait to meet her," chuckled Big Tony. "And see the photos of you in a nappy."

"If you'd both like to follow me," said the man.

Abert and Big Tony followed the man along the platform. As they walked, other passengers ran up and asked if they could have their photos taken with the little mouse and the gull.

Eventually, the man reached the coffee shop and opened the door.

"Grandma Bramble, your grandson is here," he said.

"Hello, Grandma!" said Albert, rushing in to give her a hug. "I'm sorry I am late, but the train was delayed."

"Oh, don't worry yourself. These lovely people have taken very good care of me. I was just showing them all the photos of you when you were born. I've had a lovely pot of tea and some cheese scones which are quite delicious. Would you like one?" said

Grandma Bramble, hugging her grandson back.

Albert shook his head.

"I'll have one," said the gull.

"Oh Grandma, this is my friend, Big Tony," said Albert.

"I know all about Tony. It's a pleasure to meet you. How are you?"

"I'm very well, thank you, but a bit hungry," said Big Tony, helping himself to three cheese scones and jam.

"Albert, let me look at you. Oh my, haven't you grown!" said Grandma

Bramble, turning to the station attendant. "The last time I saw Albert he could fit in the palm of my hand. Now, look at him."

The man smiled and looked at his watch.

"We had better be making our way back to the train. It is leaving again in a few minutes, Albert," he said.

Big Tony took three more cheese scones and posed for a few more photos in the coffee shop.

"This way, Mrs Bramble," said the man, opening the doors that led back out onto the platform.

"Albert! Albert! Albert!" shouted the crowd that had gathered next to the waiting train.

Albert and Big Tony signed a few more autographs and then they and Grandma Bramble got on the train.

Chapter 10

The three of them sat down in their carriage.

"It's been a real pleasure to meet you, Mrs Bramble," said the man and he then stepped down onto the platform and blew his whistle.

The train slowly started to move and several children ran alongside Albert's carriage waving.

Albert and Big Tony waved back until the train finally disappeared out of the station.

Grandma Bramble looked at Albert and smiled.

"What?" asked the little mouse.

"The children really like you, don't they?" she said.

Albert shrugged.

"Well, I'm very proud of you," said his Grandma.

"Thanks," smiled Albert.

Big Tony ate another cheese scone.

Just then there was an announcement.

"Good morning, everyone, this is your driver speaking. I'd like to welcome you all aboard the eleven fifteen from Paignton to Kingswear. I'd also like to give a very special welcome to Grandma Bramble who is on the train today. Mrs Bramble has come all the way from Scotland. As many of you will have seen we also have Albert Mouse and Big Tony on the train today so I'd like to welcome them aboard also. We are due to arrive in Kingswear at eleven thirty-five. Next stop - Kingswear."

Grandma Bramble looked at Albert again and smiled.

"Yes, I'm very proud of you, Albert," she said.

Big Tony finished off his last cheese scone and brushed the crumbs off the seat.

"Yes, the two of you have become quite the celebrities, haven't you?" Mrs Bramble said.

"Can I see those photos of Albert as a baby, please?" asked Big Tony.

"Of course, I have them right here," she said, opening her handbag and taking out a number of old photos.

"Great," muttered Albert.

"This is Albert in his little pram, and this is Albert sucking his dummy," smiled Mrs Bramble.

"Oh, I have to get myself some copies of these. I may even get some t-shirts printed," chuckled the gull.

Albert looked out of the window.

Chapter 11

At the front of the train, the driver sat back and relaxed. As the train slowly travelled past fields of cows and sheep he checked the gauges. First, he checked the brake vacuum, then the boiler pressure, the steam heating pressure and finally the water level indicator. They all looked correct.

"Time for a snack," he said, taking two rashers of bacon out of his canvas bag and placing them neatly on his coal shovel.

The driver then opened the firebox door and gently placed his shovel on the red-hot coals of the fire. From his bag, he took two slices of bread which had already been buttered.

The smell of bacon filled the air.

After a few minutes, the driver removed his shovel from the fire and closed the firebox door again. He placed the two rashers of bacon between the slices of bread and licked his lips.

He then took a large bite of his sandwich.

"Delicious!" he said, between chews.

Soon he had eaten the whole bacon sandwich.

All of a sudden he felt a tight feeling in his chest.

"Oooh, I may have eaten that a bit too quickly," he said gently tapping his chest with his hand.

But the tightness became stronger and stronger. The driver started to look worried as he struggled to catch his breath.

His head gently flopped forward and he slumped against a lever, which moved under his weight.

The train started to go faster and faster.

Chapter 12

Back in his carriage, Albert, who was still looking out of the window, noticed that the hedges seemed to be moving faster and faster past the window.

"That's odd," said the little mouse.

"What is?" asked his Grandma.

"Well, we seem to have speeded up a bit," replied Albert.

"The driver is probably late for his lunch," chuckled Big Tony. "Although I am sure I can smell a bacon sandwich in the air."

Albert sniffed the air.

"I can smell bacon too," he said.

The little mouse looked out of the window again.

"No, something is most definitely wrong," said Albert, and with that, he jumped off his seat.

"Big Tony, come with me. I think we need to investigate this," he said.

"Relax," said the gull, who was still taking deep breaths and imagining a bacon sandwich.

Then Big Tony looked out of the window as trees and fields flashed by.

"Hmmm, we do appear to be going very fast," he said.

"Oh dear, is everything going to be ok?" asked Grandma Bramble.

"Everything is going to be fine, Grandma. Big Tony and I will go and check on the driver. You stay here and don't worry."

"Be careful, Albert," she said.

Albert and Big Tony walked up the train towards the engine.

By now, other passengers had also realised that the train was travelling very fast. They looked worriedly at each other.

"There's no cause for alarm. Albert and I are going to talk to the driver and see what the problem is. Please, everyone, stay in your seats," said the gull.

Chapter 13

When Albert and Big Tony reached the front carriage, they had hoped that they would just be able to open the door and get straight into where the engine driver was, but they couldn't. Instead, they found out that the steam train was coupled up with the first carriage and there was a large open-air gap. As they looked down at the gap, they could see the tracks and sleepers whizzing by below them.

"Oops, I wasn't expecting that," said Albert, feeling a bit queasy and closing the door. "What are we going to do?"

"It's fine. I'll just fly across and have a word with the driver," said Big Tony opening the door again.

"Ok, but hurry, because it seems we are getting faster and faster. If we don't slow down soon we will be at Kingswear before we know it."

Big Tony jumped across the open gap and landed on the coal bunker.

"Wow, well done, Big Tony," said Albert.

"It was a piece of cake," said the gull as he waved to Albert and jumped down to talk to the driver.

Albert waited for Big Tony to reappear.

He waited and waited, but there was no sign of his friend.

"What's he doing in there?" Albert asked himself. "I hope everything is all right."

Chapter 14

But everything wasn't all right.

Big Tony looked at the driver who was slumped forward in his seat.

"Hey, wake up!" said the gull, tapping the man on his shoulder, but the man didn't wake up.

Big Tony tried again, screeching in the man's ear, but again there was no response. The gull looked around to see where the brake was, but he couldn't see it.

"There are so many levers and dials, I think I'd better go and fetch Albert.

He'll know what to do," the gull said to himself.

Just then he noticed the coal shovel with a few bits of burnt bacon on it. The gull picked up the shovel and held it up to his nose.

"Mmmm, bacon," he said, instantly feeling hungry, even though he had only just finished off several cheese scones.

After looking around to see if there was a half-eaten sandwich anywhere, Big Tony decided to report back to Albert.

The gull jumped back up to the coal bunker and waved at Albert.

"Phew, there you are!" said Albert. "I wondered where you'd got to. What did the driver say?"

Big Tony hopped across the gap and went into the carriage, closing the door behind him.

"The driver didn't say anything. He's asleep."

"Asleep!" asked Albert sounding horrified.

"Yup. I tried to wake him but he was stone cold fast asleep," said Big Tony. "But I was right about the bacon. Seems the driver has just had a late breakfast or an early lunch."

"Did you try and slow the train down? What about the brake?" asked the little mouse.

"I looked for it but there's no sign of it anywhere."

"Well, we need to do something because if we don't the train is just going to run out of track when it gets to Kingswear and you know what that means?" asked Albert.

"We'll crash?" replied Big Tony.

"Yes, into the sea. And I can't swim!" said Albert.

A worried look came over both their faces.

"You need to get into where the engine driver is and maybe you can see the brake," said Big Tony. "Do you think you can leap across from here onto the coal bunker?"

Albert opened the carriage door and looked at the gap. It looked even further than when he had tried leaping across the garden between the pebble and the stick when he was training for his trip to see the world.

"Jumping gaps is not really the thing I'm best at, but I'm just going to have to try," said Albert nervously.

The little mouse knew what would happen if he couldn't manage to jump across the gap and he looked at Big Tony.

"You are going to have to jump as you've never jumped before, Albert," said the gull.

"Otherwise, we are all going to be killed, even my Grandma and then my Mum will be really cross with me."

"You can do this, Albert. You're the only one who can save the train and all the passengers!" said Big Tony, slapping him on the back.

"Right, let's do it!" said Albert.

Chapter 15

Albert stepped back into the carriage and closed the door. He stood straight upright and started swinging his arms about.

"What are you doing?" asked Big Tony.

"I'm warming up like the athletes do," said Albert.

"Warming up? You don't have time to warm up! This is urgent, you need to get across that gap now or we're all going to die," said Big Tony, opening the door again.

Albert stopped warming up and stretching and took several paces backwards, and then looked at the coal bunker through the open door.

"Just don't look down," said Big Tony.

Albert could feel his knees start to shake. He knew he would only get one chance at this so he took a few more paces back and then a few more.

"Are you ready?" asked the gull.

"Ready!" called Albert, getting down on one knee and looking at the doorway.

"Three, two, one, GO!" shouted Big Tony.

Albert sprinted off down the carriage like he was in the Olympics.

"Faster, Albert, faster!" shouted Big Tony.

The little mouse ran as fast as he could down the carriage until, eventually, he reached the open doorway and he leapt as high as he could into the air.

"Don't look down Albert, don't look down!" shouted Big Tony.

The little mouse seemed to float through the air for what seemed like minutes.

A surprised look came over Albert's face, because not only did he reach the coal bunker, he flew right over it, landing with a crash on the floor next to the engine driver's feet.

Chapter 16

Big Tony's face changed from delight to horror as he saw Albert disappear into the driver's compartment.

"Oh, I do hope he hasn't landed in the fire," said the gull, trying to remember if the fire door was open or closed.

"Albert! Are you ok?" shouted the gull as he hopped across the coal bunker. "Albert, talk to me!"

The gull looked down at the floor and there was Albert trying to remove coal dust from his lovely white shirt.

"You're alive! Thank goodness," said the gull. "Are you ok, mate?"

"Yes, I think so," said Albert. "I'm a little bruised but I'll live."

"Wow, I thought you said you said jumping gaps was not the thing you were best at?"

"I wasn't," said Albert, getting to his feet.

Albert looked up at the man and it was at that moment that the little mouse saw two things of deep concern.

"Big Tony, the man isn't asleep," said Albert.

"Really? Are you sure?" asked the gull, scratching his head.

"Yes, because his eyes are open and no one sleeps with their eyes open, do they?"

"I guess not. So, what's wrong with him then?" asked Big Tony.

"I'm not sure but I've noticed he is leaning on the regulator, he must have moved it when he slipped forward."

"What's a regulator?" asked Big Tony as he jumped down onto the floor and looked up at the man.

"It's the lever that controls the speed, like an accelerator," said Albert.

"How do you know this stuff?" asked Big Tony, sounding very impressed.

"I borrowed a book on trains from Mrs Saunders at the bookshop. It was all in there," said the little mouse.

"I knew you'd know what to do."

"The first thing we need to do is push him back off the lever," said Albert climbing up the assortment of pipes, dials and gauges that the man's head was resting against.

"Ouch!" said Albert as he touched the pipe that lead to the steam pressure gauge. "That one's hot!"

The little mouse put his back against the man's head, and then placing his tiny feet against one of the dials, Albert began to push as hard as he could, but the man didn't move.

"Big Tony, get up here and give me a hand."

Big Tony hopped up next to Albert and put his back against the man's head and pushed as hard as he could too.

"That's it, Big Tony, push again. I think he's moving."

Albert was right. Slowly the man rocked backwards, back into his chair.

"Phew," said Albert. "Now all we need to do is move this regulator lever."

The two friends pushed against the lever as hard as they could. Ever so slowly the large iron lever began to move.

"Are we slowing down yet?" asked Big Tony.

"I'm not sure, but I think it might take a few minutes to slow down because we are travelling very fast."

"Albert, we don't have a few minutes!" said Big Tony.

Chapter 17

Back in her carriage, Grandma Bramble looked anxiously out of the window as were all the other passengers.

Suddenly Albert's Grandma noticed that the train was slowly reducing its speed.

"We're slowing down!" she shouted. "We're slowing down!"

Just then the train's announcement system came to life.

"Good morning, everyone, this is your driver speaking...."

"Albert?" asked Grandma Bramble, recognising her grandson's voice.

".........As I am sure you are all aware, we've been having some slight technical issues with the train's engine, but Big Tony and I have managed to get everything under control. We are due to arrive in Kingswear slightly ahead of schedule. Next stop - Kingswear," continued Albert.

He then looked at Big Tony.

"Right, I'll drive the train. Can you fly ahead to Kingswear station and tell them what's happened? Ask them to call an ambulance because I think the driver has had a heart attack."

"Heart attack?" said the gull, looking at the man. "What, because he ate a bacon sandwich?"

"I'm not sure if that caused it, but he needs help quickly," said Albert, pulling the speed lever back another notch.

"Are you sure you can drive this train?" asked Big Tony.

"I think so. I'm just glad I read that book. You fly as fast as you can, faster than you've ever flown before!"

With that, Big Tony shook Albert's hand.

"Good luck, my little friend. See you in Kingswear," and then he hopped out of the train window and flew off towards the station.

Albert checked the gauges and dials.

"The brake vacuum looks good, and so does the water level."

The little mouse moved the regulator lever as far as it would go and the large steam train began to slow even more.

"I really need to get rid of some of the steam," said the little mouse looking at the needle of the pressure gauge that was still pointing to a red mark on the dial.

Just then an idea came to him. He jumped up and grabbed the chain that was running above his head. The train's whistle sounded. Albert held onto the chain and kept pulling it. As the steam left the train's boiler through the whistle, Albert saw that the pressure gauge was slowly coming down.

"It's working!" he said excitedly.

Chapter 18

Albert looked through the small round window and up ahead he could see the station. There were lots of ambulance people and even the fire crews were there.

"Well done, Big Tony," Albert said to himself. "All I need to do is slow this train down even more."

The little mouse saw a small lever below the brake vacuum gauge.

"That must be the brake lever," he said and jumped up and pulled it.

Suddenly he could hear the sound of the brakes gripping the wheels of the train.

The train began to shake as the brakes tightened against the wheels. Albert held on to the lever and pulled as hard as he could.

Gradually the train slowed down until it came to a gentle halt alongside the platform.

"Phew, that was close," said Albert, wiping his brow.

He then pulled on the whistle chain several times.

Two of the ambulance crew climbed up the metal steps on the side of the train and stepped into the engine room.

"Hello, Albert, is this the driver?" one of them asked.

"Yes, I think he must have had a heart attack," said Albert.

"Ok, we'll take it from here," said the lady, opening up a large medical bag she was carrying, while the man checked the driver's pulse.

Albert reached for the announcement button and pressed it.

"Good morning, everyone, this is your driver speaking. Welcome to Kingswear. Please remember to take all your belongings with you when leaving the train and on behalf of Dartmouth Steam Railway and River Boat Company I'd like to thank you for travelling with us this morning. If you are crossing over to Dartmouth, then please make your way to the ferry. Thank you and goodbye."

Albert jumped down from the train.

The Station Manager ran up and hugged Albert.

"Albert Mouse, I would just like to say how grateful we all are that you've managed to save all the passengers and our train. On behalf of Dartmouth Steam Railway and River Boat Company, I'd like to offer you and Big Tony free train travel forever as a thank you. Three cheers for Albert Mouse!"

All the passengers and station staff cheered.

"Oh really, it was nothing," said Albert bowing.

Just then Big Tony walked up and stood next to Albert.

"As well as free train travel, do we get free food in your station cafe?" he asked.

"As much as you can eat!" said the manager, hugging Big Tony.

"Do they do bacon sandwiches?" the gull asked.

"The best bacon sandwiches in Kingswear!" said the manager.

"Right, Albert, I'll be in the cafe if you need me. You'd better go and help your grandma off the train," said Big Tony.

"Oh gosh, Grandma!" said Albert, who in all the excitement had forgotten about his grandmother.

The little mouse made his way along the platform, shaking hands with lots of grateful passengers. He lost count of how many times he stopped to have his photograph taken, but eventually, he reached his grandma's carriage.

"I thought you'd forgotten about me," she said.

"Never! I just had to talk to the Station Manager and things like that," said Albert, blushing.

Grandma Bramble looked around.

"Where's Big Tony?" she asked.

"Oh, he's in the cafe having his lunch. He'll probably join us at the house later," said Albert picking up Granma Bramble's suitcase. "The ferry's this way."

Before they reached the exit, Albert had to stop for several more photos. Even Grandma Bramble posed for a few.

Chapter 19

Albert and his Grandma made their way slowly down the slipway to the waiting ferry.

"Oh, a boat ride. How exciting!" said his grandmother.

"Afternoon, Albert," said the captain of the ferry. "And you must be Albert's grandma. I'm very pleased to meet you."

"Likewise," said Grandma Bramble shaking the man's hand.

"Where's Big Tony," asked the captain.

"He's just having his lunch at the moment and probably signing autographs. I suspect he will be across shortly," said Albert.

"It was amazing the way you saved all those passengers, Albert. You must be very proud of your grandson, Mrs Bramble."

"I am, but to be honest, I was proud of him even before today's exciting events," she said, smiling at Albert.

"Well, I can't promise you much excitement on this ferry trip. The waters look nice and calm."

"That's good because I think we've both had enough excitement for one day," said Grandma Bramble.

The captain was right, the water was very calm and the Tom Casey was soon on the other side of the harbour.

"Thank you so much, Mr Captain man," said Albert's grandmother as she stepped off the ferry.

"You're very welcome. Merry Christmas!"

"Oh, it is, isn't it?" said Grandma Bramble.

Albert and his grandmother walked up the slipway back towards Higher Street.

Chapter 20

The news of Albert's death-defying train rescue had already reached Dartmouth and the streets were filled with crowds of well-wishers, all eager to get a glimpse of Albert.

Even the grumpy man who had been very rude to Albert that morning was there and came across to shake Albert's hand.

"I'd just like to apologise for what I said to you this morning. Do you mind if I have a photo of us together?" he asked.

"Not at all," said Albert.

After quite a delay, Albert and his grandmother eventually made it back to No. 10 Higher Street where another large crowd had gathered. Clare at the Cherub Inn was serving lemonade and cups of tea to people who had gathered in the street waiting to welcome Albert home.

Mrs Saunders at the bookshop had sold every single copy of the books written about Albert's adventures that she had and was on the phone ordering more.

Even the local newspaper reporter was there, eager to get an exclusive interview with Albert.

They all cheered as Albert approached the house.

Albert's mother opened the garden gate and hugged her mother.

"I'm so glad you're alright," she said, crying.

"I'm fine, thanks to Albert and Big Tony. If it wasn't for them who knows where I and the other passengers would be," said Grandma Bramble.

Albert hugged his mother.

"See, Mum, I told you I'd be okay," he said.

Albert then climbed onto the garden wall and asked for everyone to be quiet for a moment.

"I have a very brief statement to make. Firstly, thank you for all coming out to welcome me home and congratulate me on saving the train. However, I couldn't have done it without the help of my friend Big Tony, who sadly can't be here at the moment as he's having his lunch. I will be speaking to reporters sometime tomorrow, but for now, I would just like to rest and spend time with my family," said Albert.

The little mouse looked down at his oily and coal-covered clothes.

"And have a wash!" he said, which made everyone laugh.

Albert waved to the crowds, then jumped off the wall and closed the gate.

He, his mother and Grandma Bramble walked slowly up the path to the house. Albert turned and gave one last wave to the crowd before stepping inside and closing the front door.

Chapter 21

Mrs Mouse went into the kitchen and put the kettle on.

"Mum, go and sit down, you must be exhausted," she said.

"Oh, I'm fine, but I suspect Albert is worn out after the day he's had?" Grandma Bramble replied.

"I am feeling a bit tired," said Albert.

"Well, you go and have a nice bath, then have a little nap. Your mother and I will be fine, won't we dear?"

Albert left Grandma Bramble chatting with his mother and went upstairs. After his bath, he went across the landing to his bedroom.

His sister's bedroom door opened.

"Albert, we saw all the people in the street. Did you really drive a train?" asked Dorothy.

"And save all those passengers, including grandma?" asked Millie.

"I certainly did," said Albert.

"Wow, you are a hero," said Dorothy, hugging her brother.

"No, I'm just Albert. Albert Mouse, pure and simple," he said closing his bedroom door.

Albert lay down on his bed and folded his arms behind his head.

"Phew, what a day. I'm worn out!" he said and slowly drifted off to sleep.

Chapter 22

While Albert was having his nap, Big Tony was finishing off his third bacon sandwich. He had a very contented look on his face and had forgotten all about Reg Rat, Stu Sparrow, Pete Pigeon and even Desmond Dog.

Big Tony said goodbye to the station staff and made his way down to the ferry. Over in Dartmouth, people were all doing their last-minute Christmas shopping but still came out of shops to congratulate him on saving the train.

"Just remember, there is only one Big Tony in Dartmouth and that's me!" he said as he posed for photos.

When he reached Higher Street Big Tony flew up to Albert's bedroom window and looked in.

"Ah, there he is, sleeping like a baby," he giggled to himself, remembering the photos that Grandma Bramble had shown him. "Sleep tight, my little friend."

Big Tony then flew up to the roof and fell asleep on one of the chimney pots.

Chapter 23

Later that afternoon, Albert yawned, stretched his little arms and legs and opened his eyes.

He then looked out of his window.

"Oh, I would have thought Big Tony would have been over to see me. I guess he's still in the cafe."

Albert then got out of bed and went downstairs.

"And this is Albert learning to walk," said Grandma Bramble, showing a photo to Dorothy and Millie.

Albert turned and walked into the kitchen, where his mother was drying the dishes.

"Did you have a nice sleep?" she asked when she saw Albert.

"I did," replied Albert yawning again. "Did I miss lunch?"

"Yes, but sit yourself down and I'll make you a cheese sandwich. Grandma brought some Scottish shortbread biscuits. You should try one, they're very good."

"Grandma's showing my baby photos to Dorothy and Millie," he sighed.

"Yes, I know," said his mother, as she cut the crusts off his sandwiches.

"She showed everyone at the station, too," said the little mouse.

"Your Grandma is very proud of you, that's all. Now, eat your sandwich. You can help me put the Christmas tree up this evening if you'd like?"

Albert nodded and picked up his sandwich.

From the lounge, Dorothy called to her mother.

"Mum, come and look at Albert in a nappy!"

Albert sighed and shook his head.

"Never mind," said Albert's mother, hugging her son.

Chapter 24

That evening Albert helped his mother put the Christmas tree up in the front window of No. 10 Higher Street.

They hung all sorts of decorations on it and finally trailed fairy lights around the tree. On the top of the tree, they placed a silver star.

As Albert, Dorothy, Millie, their mother and Grandma Bramble stood around the tree a group of carol singers gathered outside the garden gate and sang Christmas carols.

"Oh, let me go and give them some mince pies and tea. Albert, fetch my purse so I can put some money in their collection bucket," said Mrs Mouse.

"Oh, I almost forgot," said Albert, dashing upstairs to his bedroom.

After a few moments, he came downstairs and gave the five pounds back to his mother.

"Didn't you use this for the ferry trip?" asked his mother.

"No, the captain of the ferry said I didn't have to pay," replied Albert.

Mrs Mouse opened the door and gave the carol singers each a mince pie and cup of tea.

"This is from all of us," she said, putting the five-pound note in the bucket. "Merry Christmas!"

"This is the most wonderful Christmas ever," said Grandma Bramble. "Can I show the carol singers my photos of Albert as a baby?"

"No!" said Mrs Mouse.

Chapter 25

After Christmas, everything in Dartmouth returned to normal. Grandma Bramble returned to Scotland and Albert felt relieved that no one else would be seeing photos of him as a baby.

Big Tony would often go to the Station Cafe for his free food, but it wasn't half as much fun as nabbing half a pasty from an unsuspecting tourist.

As Big Tony often used to say, "I prefer to be a ducker and a diver!"

Albert did several interviews with newspapers and even the TV about how he had saved the runaway train. Although Albert always said "it was nothing really" and "anyone would have done the same", the Mayor of Dartmouth presented Albert and Big Tony with medals for their bravery.

The train driver had suffered a heart attack, but thanks to both Albert Mouse and Big Tony, and the quick actions of the medical crew, he was able to make a full recovery. Albert and Big Tony visited him in the hospital where he thanked them for saving his life.

They were also invited to the Dartmouth Visitors Centre on Mayor's Avenue to see the 'Newcomen Engine' which is the oldest working first atmospheric steam engine in the World. It was invented by a local Dartmouth man called Thomas Newcomen in 1712.

There was even talk of a steam train being named 'ALBERT'.

Several months later the people from the Guinness Book of Records measured the distance between the carriage door and where Albert had landed next to the driver and announced it was a new World Record jump for a mouse.

That made Albert very proud.

I hope you have enjoyed reading about
my adventures with
Big Tony.
If you come to Dartmouth, please come
and visit my house.
You will probably see me in my
bedroom window.
You can also join The Albert Mouse
Society

Albert 🐾🐾

GWR 5239 'GOLIATH'

GWR 5239 was designed by Charles Collett and built at the GWR Swindon Works in 1924. Its working life was spent in Neath in South Wales, until 1963 when it was sent to Barry scrapyard where it lay until 1973.

That year it was bought by the Dart Valley Railway and sent to Newton Abbot in June 1973 for restoration. Three years later it was sent to Paignton and returned to steam.

It was taken out of service on the Dartmouth Steam Railway at the end of the 2015 season and put into storage.

In 2018 it was dismantled and overhauled.

Two years later 'Goliath' was returned to the Dartmouth Steam Railway (April 2020).

Specifications

The locomotive weight is 82 long tons 2 cwt (183,900 lb or 83.4 t)

The fuel type is coal and it carries 4 long tons 0 cwt (9,000 lb or 4.1 t)

The Water capacity is 1,800 imp gal (8,200 l; 2,200 US gal)

The boiler pressure is 200 psi (1,400 kPa)

100 hundred of these trains were produced between 1923 & 1940, but now only 3 remain, one of which is 'Goliath'.

The Albert Mouse Trail

Now you can visit the places that appear in the Albert Mouse books.

Just look for these blue stickers around Dartmouth.

By Appointment to
children's imagination

If you have enjoyed this book, then please take a minute to leave a review at
www.jameshywel.com

You can also sign up for our blog to receive updates on new books from James Hywel.
https://jameshywel.com/blog

Thank you, I appreciate your support!

Acknowledgements

I'm grateful to Brian and Pam, the human owners of Cherub Cottage, for sharing their house with Albert and his family.

Thank you to the people of Dartmouth for welcoming me into their vibrant town which holds an abundance of charm and seafaring history.

As always I am grateful to "Walter" for sending me the breeze that moves the willows.

About James Hywel

James Hywel is a children's author and creator
of both Mr Milliner and Albert Mouse.
He has written over twenty books.

He is a member of *The Royal Society of Literature*
and *The Society of Authors*.

For more books and updates:

www.jameshywel.com

Printed in Great Britain
by Amazon

20105169R00081